G000019598

THIS JOURNAL BELONGS TO

THE
BIRD WATCHER'S
JOURNAL

HOW TO USE THIS BOOK

WELCOME TO YOUR BIRD WATCHING JOURNAL, a place to effectively track your experiences, improve your birding skills, and record fond memories to look back on.

This field notebook is divided into three parts. First are the Bird Watching Logs, which are the heart of the journal. Here, you have a place to record details about specific outings. Each log entry includes prompts for key information, such as the date, location, time of day, habitat, and weather. Use the notes section to record whom you were with or unique aspects of the day. A grid is provided to record the birds you've identified, and the ones you cannot. By recording the description and behavior of birds you don't recognize, you can use that information to look them up later. Each log also includes a blank space for sketches and a place to document photography or video you may have taken during your outing. Designate a Log # for each session to correlate with your entries in the Bird Watching Log Index found on pages 6–9. This way, every excursion will be easy to find and reference.

Following the logs, there's a section with blank pages for you to include additional notes or drawings—map your favorite bird-spotting locale, sketch your favorite birds, or just reminisce about a particularly memorable experience.

The final section, Birding Lists, gives you a place to keep tabs on the birds found in your own backyard, a wish list of birds you hope to see someday, and a bucket list of bird watching destinations.

HAPPY BIRD WATCHING!

BIRD WATCHING LOGS

BIRD WATCHING LOG INDEX

LOG #	LOCATION	DATE

LOG #	LOCATION	DATE

BIRD WATCHING LOG INDEX

LOG #	LOCATION	DATE

LOG #	LOCATION	DATE

BIRD WATCHING LOG LOG

DATE

LOCATION

START TIME

END TIME

HABITAT

WEATHER

NOTES ON THE DAY

SKETCHES

BIRDS I SAW

NAME/DESCRIPTION	DETAILS/BEHAVIOR

PICTURES/VIDEOS I TOOK (file name) _____

_____

_____

_____

OVERALL RATING OF THE DAY

BIRD WATCHING LOG LOG

DATE　　　　　　　　**LOCATION**

START TIME　　　　　　**END TIME**

HABITAT　　　　　　　**WEATHER**

NOTES ON THE DAY

SKETCHES

BIRDS I SAW

NAME/DESCRIPTION	DETAILS/BEHAVIOR

PICTURES/VIDEOS I TOOK (file name) _____

_____

_____

_____

OVERALL RATING OF THE DAY

BIRD WATCHING LOG

LOG #

DATE

LOCATION

START TIME

END TIME

HABITAT

WEATHER

NOTES ON THE DAY

SKETCHES

BIRDS I SAW

NAME/DESCRIPTION	DETAILS/BEHAVIOR

PICTURES/VIDEOS I TOOK (file name) _____

_____

_____

_____

OVERALL RATING OF THE DAY

BIRD WATCHING LOG

LOG #

DATE

LOCATION

START TIME

END TIME

HABITAT

WEATHER

NOTES ON THE DAY

SKETCHES

BIRDS I SAW

NAME/DESCRIPTION	DETAILS/BEHAVIOR

PICTURES/VIDEOS I TOOK (file name) _____

_____

_____

_____

OVERALL RATING OF THE DAY

 **BIRD WATCHING LOG** LOG #

DATE

LOCATION

START TIME

END TIME

HABITAT

WEATHER

NOTES ON THE DAY

SKETCHES

BIRDS I SAW

NAME/DESCRIPTION	DETAILS/BEHAVIOR

PICTURES/VIDEOS I TOOK (file name) _____

_____

_____

_____

OVERALL RATING OF THE DAY

BIRD WATCHING LOG LOG

DATE

LOCATION

START TIME

END TIME

HABITAT

WEATHER

NOTES ON THE DAY

SKETCHES

BIRDS I SAW

NAME/DESCRIPTION	DETAILS/BEHAVIOR

PICTURES/VIDEOS I TOOK (file name) _____

_____

_____

_____

OVERALL RATING OF THE DAY

BIRD WATCHING LOG

LOG #

DATE

LOCATION

START TIME

END TIME

HABITAT

WEATHER

NOTES ON THE DAY

SKETCHES

BIRDS I SAW

NAME/DESCRIPTION	DETAILS/BEHAVIOR

PICTURES/VIDEOS I TOOK (file name) _____

_____

_____

_____

OVERALL RATING OF THE DAY

BIRD WATCHING LOG

LOG #

DATE

LOCATION

START TIME

END TIME

HABITAT

WEATHER

NOTES ON THE DAY

SKETCHES

BIRDS I SAW

NAME/DESCRIPTION	DETAILS/BEHAVIOR

PICTURES/VIDEOS I TOOK (file name) _____

_____

_____

_____

OVERALL RATING OF THE DAY

BIRD WATCHING LOG

LOG #

DATE

LOCATION

START TIME

END TIME

HABITAT

WEATHER

NOTES ON THE DAY

SKETCHES

BIRDS I SAW

NAME/DESCRIPTION	DETAILS/BEHAVIOR

PICTURES/VIDEOS I TOOK (file name) _____

_____

_____

_____

OVERALL RATING OF THE DAY

BIRD WATCHING LOG

LOG #

DATE

LOCATION

START TIME

END TIME

HABITAT

WEATHER

NOTES ON THE DAY _____

_____

_____

_____

SKETCHES

BIRDS I SAW

NAME/DESCRIPTION	DETAILS/BEHAVIOR

PICTURES/VIDEOS I TOOK (file name) _____

_____

_____

_____

OVERALL RATING OF THE DAY

BIRD WATCHING LOG

LOG #

DATE

LOCATION

START TIME

END TIME

HABITAT

WEATHER

NOTES ON THE DAY

SKETCHES

BIRDS I SAW

NAME/DESCRIPTION	DETAILS/BEHAVIOR

PICTURES/VIDEOS I TOOK (file name) _____

_____

_____

_____

OVERALL RATING OF THE DAY

BIRD WATCHING LOG

LOG #

DATE

LOCATION

START TIME

END TIME

HABITAT

WEATHER

NOTES ON THE DAY

SKETCHES

BIRDS I SAW

NAME/DESCRIPTION	DETAILS/BEHAVIOR

PICTURES/VIDEOS I TOOK (file name) _____

_____

_____

_____

OVERALL RATING OF THE DAY

BIRD WATCHING LOG

LOG #

DATE

LOCATION

START TIME

END TIME

HABITAT

WEATHER

NOTES ON THE DAY

SKETCHES

BIRDS I SAW

NAME/DESCRIPTION	DETAILS/BEHAVIOR

PICTURES/VIDEOS I TOOK (file name) _____

_____

_____

_____

OVERALL RATING OF THE DAY

BIRD WATCHING LOG

LOG #

DATE

LOCATION

START TIME

END TIME

HABITAT

WEATHER

NOTES ON THE DAY

SKETCHES

BIRDS I SAW

NAME/DESCRIPTION	DETAILS/BEHAVIOR

PICTURES/VIDEOS I TOOK (file name) _____

_____

_____

_____

OVERALL RATING OF THE DAY

BIRD WATCHING LOG

LOG #

DATE

LOCATION

START TIME

END TIME

HABITAT

WEATHER

NOTES ON THE DAY

SKETCHES

BIRDS I SAW

NAME/DESCRIPTION	DETAILS/BEHAVIOR

PICTURES/VIDEOS I TOOK (file name) _____

_____

_____

_____

OVERALL RATING OF THE DAY

BIRD WATCHING LOG   LOG

DATE   **LOCATION**

START TIME   **END TIME**

HABITAT   **WEATHER**

NOTES ON THE DAY

SKETCHES

BIRDS I SAW

NAME/DESCRIPTION	DETAILS/BEHAVIOR

PICTURES/VIDEOS I TOOK (file name) _____

_____

_____

_____

OVERALL RATING OF THE DAY

BIRD WATCHING LOG LOG #

DATE

LOCATION

START TIME

END TIME

HABITAT

WEATHER

NOTES ON THE DAY

SKETCHES

BIRDS I SAW

NAME/DESCRIPTION	DETAILS/BEHAVIOR

PICTURES/VIDEOS I TOOK (file name) _____

_____

_____

_____

OVERALL RATING OF THE DAY

 **BIRD WATCHING LOG** LOG #

DATE

LOCATION

START TIME

END TIME

HABITAT

WEATHER

NOTES ON THE DAY

SKETCHES

BIRDS I SAW

NAME/DESCRIPTION	DETAILS/BEHAVIOR

PICTURES/VIDEOS I TOOK (file name) _____

_____

_____

_____

OVERALL RATING OF THE DAY

 # BIRD WATCHING LOG

LOG #

DATE

LOCATION

START TIME

END TIME

HABITAT

WEATHER

NOTES ON THE DAY

SKETCHES

BIRDS I SAW

NAME/DESCRIPTION	DETAILS/BEHAVIOR

PICTURES/VIDEOS I TOOK (file name) _____

_____

_____

_____

OVERALL RATING OF THE DAY

BIRD WATCHING LOG

LOG #

DATE

LOCATION

START TIME

END TIME

HABITAT

WEATHER

NOTES ON THE DAY

SKETCHES

BIRDS I SAW

NAME/DESCRIPTION	DETAILS/BEHAVIOR

PICTURES/VIDEOS I TOOK (file name) _____

_____

_____

_____

OVERALL RATING OF THE DAY

BIRD WATCHING LOG LOG #

DATE

LOCATION

START TIME

END TIME

HABITAT

WEATHER

NOTES ON THE DAY

SKETCHES

BIRDS I SAW

NAME/DESCRIPTION	DETAILS/BEHAVIOR

PICTURES/VIDEOS I TOOK (file name) _____

_____

_____

_____

OVERALL RATING OF THE DAY

BIRD WATCHING LOG LOG #

DATE

LOCATION

START TIME

END TIME

HABITAT

WEATHER

NOTES ON THE DAY

SKETCHES

BIRDS I SAW

NAME/DESCRIPTION	DETAILS/BEHAVIOR

PICTURES/VIDEOS I TOOK (file name) _____

_____

_____

_____

OVERALL RATING OF THE DAY

BIRD WATCHING LOG

LOG #

DATE

LOCATION

START TIME

END TIME

HABITAT

WEATHER

NOTES ON THE DAY

SKETCHES

BIRDS I SAW

NAME/DESCRIPTION	DETAILS/BEHAVIOR

PICTURES/VIDEOS I TOOK (file name) _____

_____

_____

_____

OVERALL RATING OF THE DAY

BIRD WATCHING LOG

LOG #

DATE

LOCATION

START TIME

END TIME

HABITAT

WEATHER

NOTES ON THE DAY

SKETCHES

BIRDS I SAW

NAME/DESCRIPTION	DETAILS/BEHAVIOR

PICTURES/VIDEOS I TOOK (file name) _____

_____

_____

_____

OVERALL RATING OF THE DAY

BIRD WATCHING LOG

LOG #

DATE

LOCATION

START TIME

END TIME

HABITAT

WEATHER

NOTES ON THE DAY

SKETCHES

BIRDS I SAW

NAME/DESCRIPTION	DETAILS/BEHAVIOR

PICTURES/VIDEOS I TOOK (file name) _____

_____

_____

_____

OVERALL RATING OF THE DAY

BIRD WATCHING LOG

LOG #

DATE

LOCATION

START TIME

END TIME

HABITAT

WEATHER

NOTES ON THE DAY

SKETCHES

BIRDS I SAW

NAME/DESCRIPTION	DETAILS/BEHAVIOR

PICTURES/VIDEOS I TOOK (file name) _____

_____

_____

_____

OVERALL RATING OF THE DAY

BIRD WATCHING LOG

LOG #

DATE

LOCATION

START TIME

END TIME

HABITAT

WEATHER

NOTES ON THE DAY

SKETCHES

BIRDS I SAW

NAME/DESCRIPTION	DETAILS/BEHAVIOR

PICTURES/VIDEOS I TOOK (file name) _____

_____

_____

_____

OVERALL RATING OF THE DAY

BIRD WATCHING LOG | LOG #

DATE

LOCATION

START TIME

END TIME

HABITAT

WEATHER

NOTES ON THE DAY _____

_____

_____

_____

SKETCHES

BIRDS I SAW

NAME/DESCRIPTION	DETAILS/BEHAVIOR

PICTURES/VIDEOS I TOOK (file name) _____

_____

_____

_____

OVERALL RATING OF THE DAY

BIRD WATCHING LOG   LOG

DATE

LOCATION

START TIME

END TIME

HABITAT

WEATHER

NOTES ON THE DAY

SKETCHES

BIRDS I SAW

NAME/DESCRIPTION	DETAILS/BEHAVIOR

PICTURES/VIDEOS I TOOK (file name) _____

_____

_____

_____

OVERALL RATING OF THE DAY

BIRD WATCHING LOG

LOG #

DATE

LOCATION

START TIME

END TIME

HABITAT

WEATHER

NOTES ON THE DAY

SKETCHES

BIRDS I SAW

NAME/DESCRIPTION	DETAILS/BEHAVIOR

PICTURES/VIDEOS I TOOK (file name) _____

_____

_____

_____

OVERALL RATING OF THE DAY

BIRD WATCHING LOG LOG #

DATE

LOCATION

START TIME

END TIME

HABITAT

WEATHER

NOTES ON THE DAY _____

_____

_____

_____

SKETCHES

BIRDS I SAW

NAME/DESCRIPTION	DETAILS/BEHAVIOR

PICTURES/VIDEOS I TOOK (file name) _____

_____

_____

_____

OVERALL RATING OF THE DAY

BIRD WATCHING LOG LOG

DATE

LOCATION

START TIME

END TIME

HABITAT

WEATHER

NOTES ON THE DAY

SKETCHES

BIRDS I SAW

NAME/DESCRIPTION	DETAILS/BEHAVIOR

PICTURES/VIDEOS I TOOK (file name) _____

_____

_____

_____

OVERALL RATING OF THE DAY

BIRD WATCHING LOG LOG

DATE

LOCATION

START TIME

END TIME

HABITAT

WEATHER

NOTES ON THE DAY

SKETCHES

BIRDS I SAW

NAME/DESCRIPTION	DETAILS/BEHAVIOR

PICTURES/VIDEOS I TOOK (file name) _____

_____

_____

_____

OVERALL RATING OF THE DAY

BIRD WATCHING LOG LOG #

DATE

LOCATION

START TIME

END TIME

HABITAT

WEATHER

NOTES ON THE DAY

SKETCHES

BIRDS I SAW

NAME/DESCRIPTION	DETAILS/BEHAVIOR

PICTURES/VIDEOS I TOOK (file name)

OVERALL RATING OF THE DAY

BIRD WATCHING LOG

LOG #

DATE

LOCATION

START TIME

END TIME

HABITAT

WEATHER

NOTES ON THE DAY

SKETCHES

BIRDS I SAW

NAME/DESCRIPTION	DETAILS/BEHAVIOR

PICTURES/VIDEOS I TOOK (file name) _____

_____

_____

_____

OVERALL RATING OF THE DAY

BIRD WATCHING LOG — LOG

DATE

LOCATION

START TIME

END TIME

HABITAT

WEATHER

NOTES ON THE DAY

SKETCHES

BIRDS I SAW

NAME/DESCRIPTION	DETAILS/BEHAVIOR

PICTURES/VIDEOS I TOOK (file name) _____

_____

_____

_____

OVERALL RATING OF THE DAY

BIRD WATCHING LOG

LOG #

DATE

LOCATION

START TIME

END TIME

HABITAT

WEATHER

NOTES ON THE DAY

SKETCHES

BIRDS I SAW

NAME/DESCRIPTION	DETAILS/BEHAVIOR

PICTURES/VIDEOS I TOOK (file name) _____

_____

_____

_____

OVERALL RATING OF THE DAY

BIRD WATCHING LOG

LOG #

DATE

LOCATION

START TIME

END TIME

HABITAT

WEATHER

NOTES ON THE DAY

SKETCHES

BIRDS I SAW

NAME/DESCRIPTION	DETAILS/BEHAVIOR

PICTURES/VIDEOS I TOOK (file name) _____

_____

_____

_____

OVERALL RATING OF THE DAY

BIRD WATCHING LOG

LOG #

DATE

LOCATION

START TIME

END TIME

HABITAT

WEATHER

NOTES ON THE DAY _____

_____

_____

_____

SKETCHES

BIRDS I SAW

NAME/DESCRIPTION	DETAILS/BEHAVIOR

PICTURES/VIDEOS I TOOK (file name) _____

_____

_____

_____

OVERALL RATING OF THE DAY

BIRD WATCHING LOG

LOG #

DATE

LOCATION

START TIME

END TIME

HABITAT

WEATHER

NOTES ON THE DAY

SKETCHES

BIRDS I SAW

NAME/DESCRIPTION	DETAILS/BEHAVIOR

PICTURES/VIDEOS I TOOK (file name) _____

_____

_____

_____

OVERALL RATING OF THE DAY

BIRD WATCHING LOG LOG

DATE

LOCATION

START TIME

END TIME

HABITAT

WEATHER

NOTES ON THE DAY

SKETCHES

BIRDS I SAW

NAME/DESCRIPTION	DETAILS/BEHAVIOR

PICTURES/VIDEOS I TOOK (file name) _____

_____

_____

_____

OVERALL RATING OF THE DAY

BIRD WATCHING LOG

LOG #

DATE

LOCATION

START TIME

END TIME

HABITAT

WEATHER

NOTES ON THE DAY

SKETCHES

BIRDS I SAW

NAME/DESCRIPTION	DETAILS/BEHAVIOR

PICTURES/VIDEOS I TOOK (file name) _____

_____

_____

_____

OVERALL RATING OF THE DAY

BIRD WATCHING LOG

LOG #

DATE

LOCATION

START TIME

END TIME

HABITAT

WEATHER

NOTES ON THE DAY

SKETCHES

BIRDS I SAW

NAME/DESCRIPTION	DETAILS/BEHAVIOR

PICTURES/VIDEOS I TOOK (file name) _____

_____

_____

_____

OVERALL RATING OF THE DAY

 **BIRD WATCHING LOG** LOG #

DATE

LOCATION

START TIME

END TIME

HABITAT

WEATHER

NOTES ON THE DAY

SKETCHES

BIRDS I SAW

NAME/DESCRIPTION	DETAILS/BEHAVIOR

PICTURES/VIDEOS I TOOK (file name) _____

_____

_____

_____

OVERALL RATING OF THE DAY

 **BIRD WATCHING LOG** LOG #

DATE

LOCATION

START TIME

END TIME

HABITAT

WEATHER

NOTES ON THE DAY

SKETCHES

BIRDS I SAW

NAME/DESCRIPTION	DETAILS/BEHAVIOR

PICTURES/VIDEOS I TOOK (file name) _____

_____

_____

_____

OVERALL RATING OF THE DAY

BIRD WATCHING LOG
LOG #

DATE

LOCATION

START TIME

END TIME

HABITAT

WEATHER

NOTES ON THE DAY

SKETCHES

BIRDS I SAW

NAME/DESCRIPTION	DETAILS/BEHAVIOR

PICTURES/VIDEOS I TOOK (file name) _____

_____

_____

_____

OVERALL RATING OF THE DAY

BIRD WATCHING LOG

LOG #

DATE

LOCATION

START TIME

END TIME

HABITAT

WEATHER

NOTES ON THE DAY

SKETCHES

BIRDS I SAW

NAME/DESCRIPTION	DETAILS/BEHAVIOR

PICTURES/VIDEOS I TOOK (file name) _____

_____

_____

_____

OVERALL RATING OF THE DAY

BIRD WATCHING LOG   LOG

DATE   LOCATION

START TIME   END TIME

HABITAT   WEATHER

NOTES ON THE DAY

SKETCHES

BIRDS I SAW

NAME/DESCRIPTION	DETAILS/BEHAVIOR

PICTURES/VIDEOS I TOOK (file name) _____

_____

_____

_____

OVERALL RATING OF THE DAY

BIRD WATCHING LOG

LOG #

DATE

LOCATION

START TIME

END TIME

HABITAT

WEATHER

NOTES ON THE DAY _____

_____

_____

_____

SKETCHES

BIRDS I SAW

NAME/DESCRIPTION	DETAILS/BEHAVIOR

PICTURES/VIDEOS I TOOK (file name) _____

_____

_____

_____

OVERALL RATING OF THE DAY

BIRD WATCHING LOG LOG #

DATE

LOCATION

START TIME

END TIME

HABITAT

WEATHER

NOTES ON THE DAY

SKETCHES

BIRDS I SAW

NAME/DESCRIPTION	DETAILS/BEHAVIOR

PICTURES/VIDEOS I TOOK (file name) _____

_____

_____

_____

OVERALL RATING OF THE DAY

BIRD WATCHING LOG

LOG #

DATE

LOCATION

START TIME

END TIME

HABITAT

WEATHER

NOTES ON THE DAY _____

_____

_____

_____

SKETCHES

BIRDS I SAW

NAME/DESCRIPTION	DETAILS/BEHAVIOR

PICTURES/VIDEOS I TOOK (file name) _____

_____

_____

_____

OVERALL RATING OF THE DAY

BIRD WATCHING LOG   LOG

DATE

LOCATION

START TIME

END TIME

HABITAT

WEATHER

NOTES ON THE DAY _____

SKETCHES

BIRDS I SAW

NAME/DESCRIPTION	DETAILS/BEHAVIOR

PICTURES/VIDEOS I TOOK (file name) _____

_____

_____

_____

OVERALL RATING OF THE DAY

BIRD WATCHING LOG

LOG #

DATE

LOCATION

START TIME

END TIME

HABITAT

WEATHER

NOTES ON THE DAY

SKETCHES

BIRDS I SAW

NAME/DESCRIPTION	DETAILS/BEHAVIOR

PICTURES/VIDEOS I TOOK (file name) _____

_____

_____

_____

OVERALL RATING OF THE DAY

NOTES & SKETCHES

"WHEREVER THERE ARE BIRDS, THERE IS HOPE."

—Mehmet Murat Ildan

"TO SIT IN THE SHADE ON A FINE DAY AND LOOK UPON
VERDURE IS THE MOST PERFECT REFRESHMENT."

—Jane Austen

"THE BLUEBIRD CARRIES THE SKY ON HIS BACK."

—Henry David Thoreau

"NOTHING IN THE WORLD IS QUITE AS ADORABLY
LOVELY AS A ROBIN WHEN HE SHOWS OFF—
AND THEY ARE NEARLY ALWAYS DOING IT."

—Frances Hodgson Burnett

"IN ORDER TO SEE BIRDS, IT IS NECESSARY
TO BECOME PART OF THE SILENCE."

—Robert Wilson Lynd

"BIRDS ARE A MIRACLE BECAUSE THEY PROVE
TO US THERE IS A FINER, SIMPLER STATE OF
BEING WHICH WE MAY STRIVE TO ATTAIN."

—Douglas Coupland

"MAY MY HEART ALWAYS BE OPEN TO LITTLE BIRDS
WHO ARE THE SECRETS OF LIVING."

—E. E. Cummings

"A BIRDSONG CAN, EVEN FOR A MOMENT, MAKE THE WHOLE WORLD INTO A SKY WITHIN US, BECAUSE WE FEEL THAT THE BIRD DOES NOT DISTINGUISH BETWEEN ITS HEART AND THE WORLD'S."

—Rainer Maria Rilke

"IF I HAD TO CHOOSE, I WOULD RATHER HAVE BIRDS THAN AIRPLANES."
—Charles Lindbergh

"BIRDS WILL GIVE YOU A WINDOW, IF YOU ALLOW THEM. THEY WILL SHOW YOU SECRETS FROM ANOTHER WORLD, FRESH VISIONS THAT, ALTHOUGH AVIAN, CAN ACCOMPANY YOU HOME AND ALTER YOUR LIFE."

—Lyanda Lynn Haupt

BIRDING LISTS

BACKYARD BIRDING

SOMETIMES THE MOST MEMORABLE BIRD WATCHING experiences occur from our own window or patio. Compile a list here of the birds you have enjoyed observing in your own backyard.

BIRD	DATE/TIME	NOTES

MY BIRDING WISH LIST

THERE ARE AN ESTIMATED 9,000 TO 10,000 SPECIES of birds in the world, ranging from the bizarre and intriguing to the colorful and majestic. Record the birds you hope to see in your lifetime here, and check them off when you are lucky enough to spot them.

- [ ] _____
- [ ] _____
- [ ] _____
- [ ] _____
- [ ] _____
- [ ] _____
- [ ] _____
- [ ] _____
- [ ] _____
- [ ] _____
- [ ] _____
- [ ] _____
- [ ] _____
- [ ] _____
- [ ] _____
- [ ] _____
- [ ] _____
- [ ] _____

MY BIRD-WATCHING DESTINATIONS

FROM WILDLIFE REFUGES TO NATIONAL PARKS,
there are so many worthy places across the globe ripe for bird watching.
Are there places you hope to travel to see a particular species of bird?
Keep the details here.

DESTINATION   **SEASON**

BIRD(S) I HOPE TO ENCOUNTER _____

_____

_____

NOTES _____

_____

_____ ☐ **TRIP PLANNED**

DESTINATION   **SEASON**

BIRD(S) I HOPE TO ENCOUNTER _____

_____

_____

NOTES _____

_____

_____ ☐ **TRIP PLANNED**

DESTINATION **SEASON**

BIRD(S) I HOPE TO ENCOUNTER

NOTES

☐ TRIP PLANNED

DESTINATION **SEASON**

BIRD(S) I HOPE TO ENCOUNTER

NOTES

☐ TRIP PLANNED

DESTINATION **SEASON**

BIRD(S) I HOPE TO ENCOUNTER

NOTES

☐ TRIP PLANNED

THE
BIRD WATCHER'S
JOURNAL

weldon**owen**

www.weldonowen.com

© 2022 Weldon Owen International. All rights reserved.

ISBN: 978-1-68188-865-1

PRINTED IN CHINA

10 9 8 7 6 5 4 3 2 1